Create and Share | Thinking Digitally

Creating Digital Videos

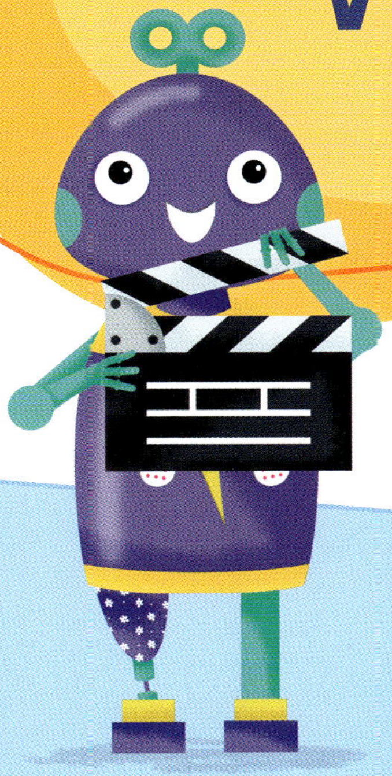

By Amber Lovett

Published in the United States of America by:
CHERRY LAKE PRESS
2395 South Huron Parkway, Suite 200, Ann Arbor, Michigan
www.cherrylakepublishing.com

Series Adviser: Kristin Fontichiaro
Reading Adviser: Marla Conn, MS, Ed., Literacy specialist, Read-Ability, Inc.
Book Designer: Felicia Macheske
Character Illustrator: Rachael McLean

Photo Credits: © Dmytro Zinkevych/Shutterstock.com, 7; © Marina Onokhina/Shutterstock.com, 13

Graphics Throughout: © the simple surface/Shutterstock.com; © Diana Rich/Shutterstock.com; © lemony/Shutterstock.com; © CojoMoxon/Shutterstock.com; © IreneArt/Shutterstock.com; © Artefficient/Shutterstock.com; © Marie Nimrichterova/Shutterstock.com; © Svetolk/Shutterstock.com; © EV-DA/Shutterstock.com; © briddy/Shutterstock.com; © Mix3r/Shutterstock.com

Library of Congress Cataloging-in-Publication Data

Names: Lovett, Amber, author. | McLean, Rachael, illustrator.
Title: Creating digital videos / by Amber Lovett ; illustrated by Rachael McLean.
Description: Ann Arbor, Michigan : Cherry Lake Publishing, 2020. | Series: Create and share : thinking digitally | Includes index. | Audience: Grades 2-3.
Identifiers: LCCN 2019033454 | ISBN 9781534159129 (hardcover) | ISBN 9781534161429 (paperback) | ISBN 9781534160279 (pdf) | ISBN 9781534162570 (ebook)
Subjects: LCSH: Digital cinematography—Juvenile literature. | Digital video—Juvenile literature. | Video recording—Juvenile literature.
Classification: LCC TR860 .L68 2020 | DDC 777—dc23
LC record available at https://lccn.loc.gov/2019033454

Cherry Lake Publishing would like to acknowledge the work of the Partnership for 21st Century Learning, a Network of Battelle for Kids. Please visit *www.battelleforkids.org/networks/p21* for more information.

Printed in the United States of America
Corporate Graphics

CHERRY LAKE PRESS

Table of
CONTENTS

CHAPTER ONE

Plan Your Video

Watching videos is fun. But did you know that filming one can be fun too? There are a lot of ways to film a video. All you need is a camera or smartphone and a computer.

The first thing to think about is who will watch your video. This is called your **audience**. What kind of movie will your audience want to see? Should your movie be about real information and facts? Or do you want to tell your audience a story?

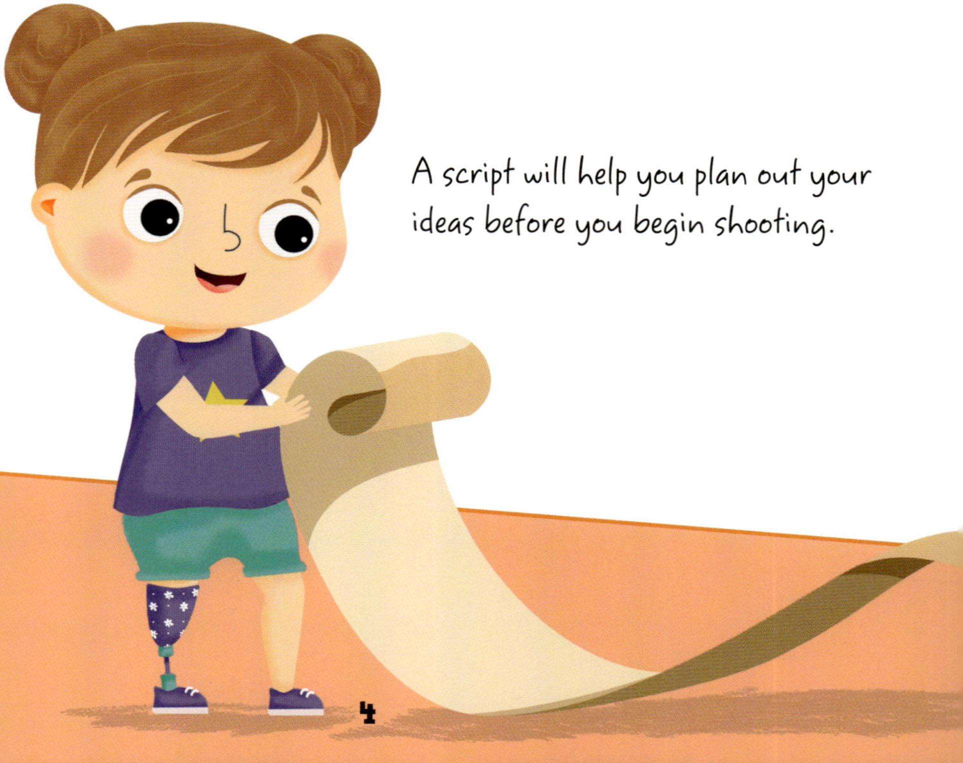

A script will help you plan out your ideas before you begin shooting.

Next, think about what and who you will film. You can make videos with people, called actors. You can make videos using **inanimate** objects, like a toy car or teddy bear. You can also make video diaries, called video blogs, or vlogs. In vlogs, you talk directly to the audience.

Now you know what kind of video you want to shoot. Next, think about what will happen in your video. Your video will need a beginning, a middle, and an end. Write down what will happen in each part of your video. You might also want to write a **script**. A script tells the actors every word they will say. It also provides a plan for what will happen in the story.

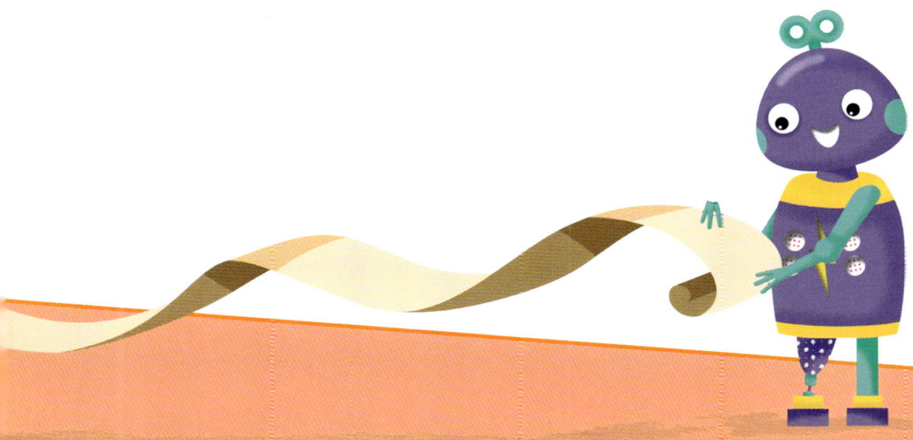

Last, you must plan your **shots**. You can do this by creating a **storyboard**. Think about how each part of your video will look, feel, and sound. Different shots and angles have different effects. They can give your movie a different feel. Long shots show a person's whole body. Close-up shots only show the face and shoulders. Try to film from different angles: from the front, from the side, or from above. Each new shot can change the **mood** of your video.

Many famous YouTubers make video blogs, or vlogs. Some vlogs review new products. Other vlogs teach you how to do something. What are your favorite vlogs to watch?

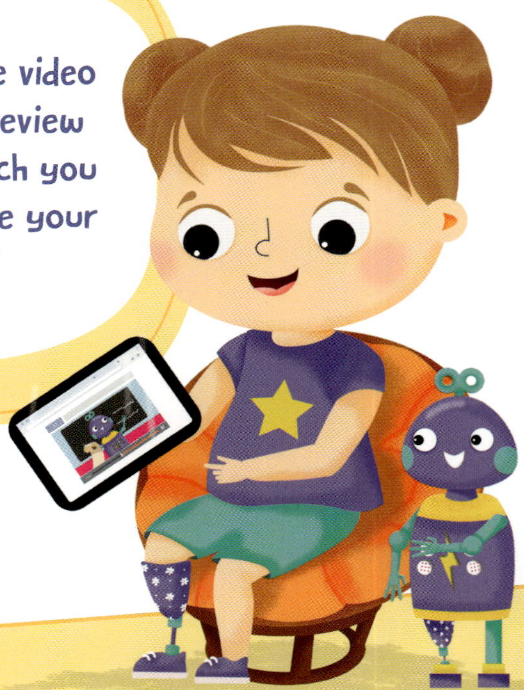

ACTIVITY

Storyboard

Create a storyboard for your video. Follow these steps to get started.

1. Decide how many different **scenes**, or shots, your video will have.
2. Draw a box for each scene.
3. Draw a picture in each box to show what your scene will look like.
4. Write a short sentence underneath each box describing the scene.
5. Use your storyboard to help you shoot your video.

What type of video would you want to film?

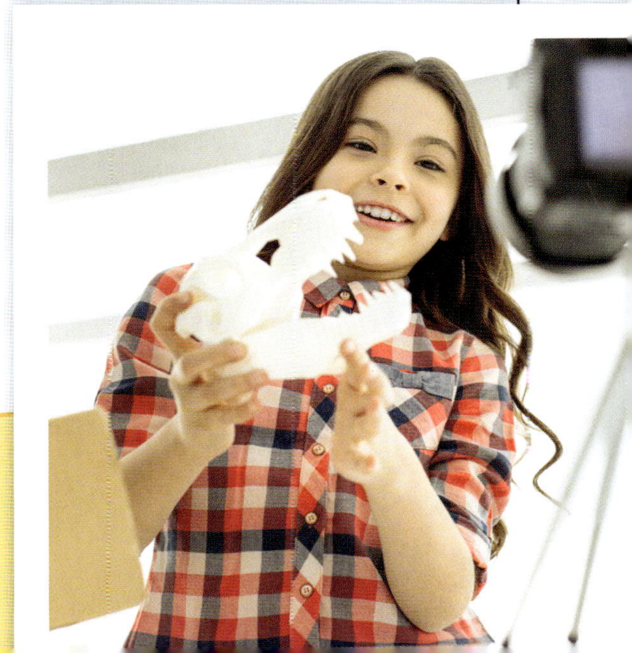

CHAPTER TWO

Shoot Your Video

Now that you have a plan for your video, you can start filming! You will need a camera that can record video. If your parents have a video camera, ask if you can use it. You can also shoot your video using a smartphone. Before you start filming, ask an adult to show you how to use the camera. Make sure you know how to record, stop the video, and play it back.

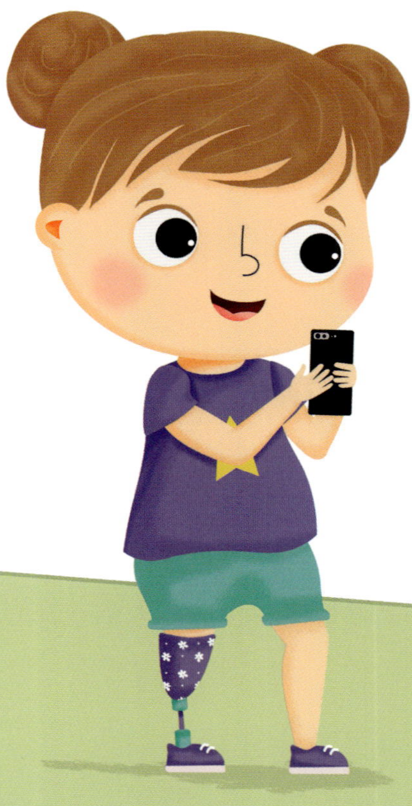

Before you film, check to make sure your camera has enough light to show a clear picture. If the room you film in is too dark, your movie might be hard to see. Try to add more light to a room. Or go outside to film if it is too dark inside. Make sure that you film in a quiet place. You don't want loud sounds or too many noises in the background. Then it will be hard to hear your actors.

Shoot all the scenes you will need in your video. Use your storyboard as a guide. It's a good idea to shoot the same scene more than one time. Maybe have your actors act out the same scene differently. When you edit your video, you can go back and pick out the best scenes to use.

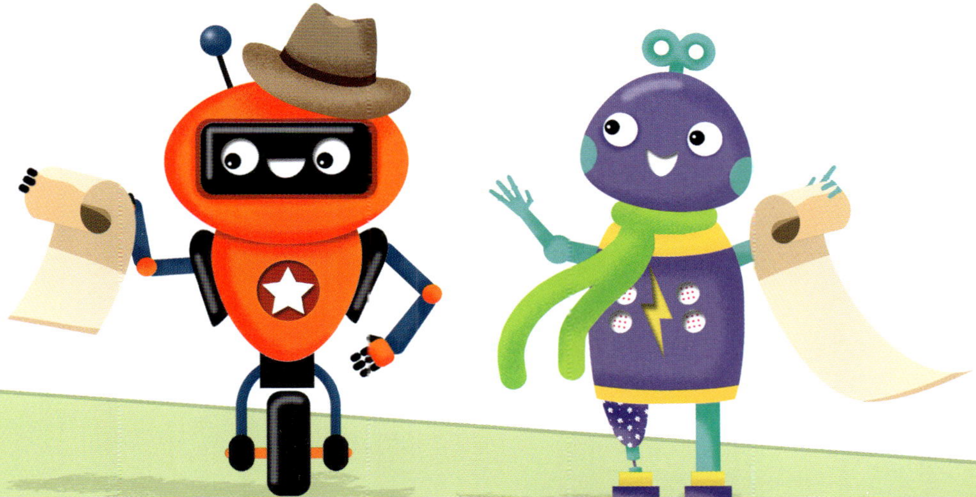

ACTIVITY

Filming

Before you start filming, make sure you have everything you need before heading to your location.

THINGS TO BRING:

- Script and storyboard
- Actors or inanimate objects
- **Props**, like a cowboy hat or scarf
- Friends to help film

Once you have everything you need, it's time to film!

Reshoot any parts of your video that weren't right the first time.

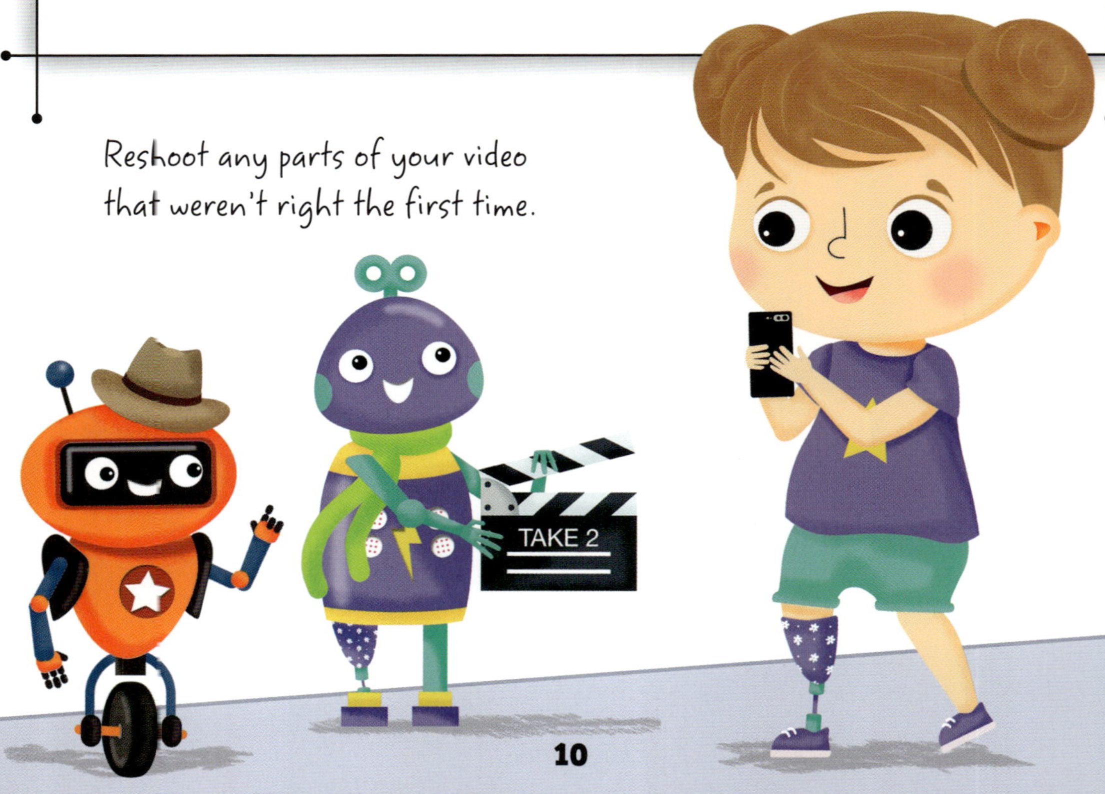

ACTIVITY
-Continued-

INSTRUCTIONS:

1. Ask an adult to help you find a camera you can use to shoot your video. Ask how to use the camera if you need help!
2. Grab the actors for your film and find a quiet space to record.
3. Now, try to film the first scene from your storyboard.
4. Play your scene back to see how it looks. Do you need to record it again? You can record the same scene as many times as you need to.
5. Once you are happy with your first scene, go on to the second. Keep filming it until it looks right.
6. Keep going! Check off each scene as you film so you know when you are done.
7. Whew! You filmed your video. Let's go to the next step!

TIP: Sometimes you may need to film your video out of **sequence**, especially if you're filming in different locations! Do the beginning and ending of your video take place in the same location? If so, you might want to film those two scenes first. You can rearrange the scenes in order later when you edit your video.

If you are shooting a vlog, you might not need to shoot in scenes. Instead, practice recording yourself talking to the camera. Look right at the camera. Speak loudly and slowly so everyone can understand you.

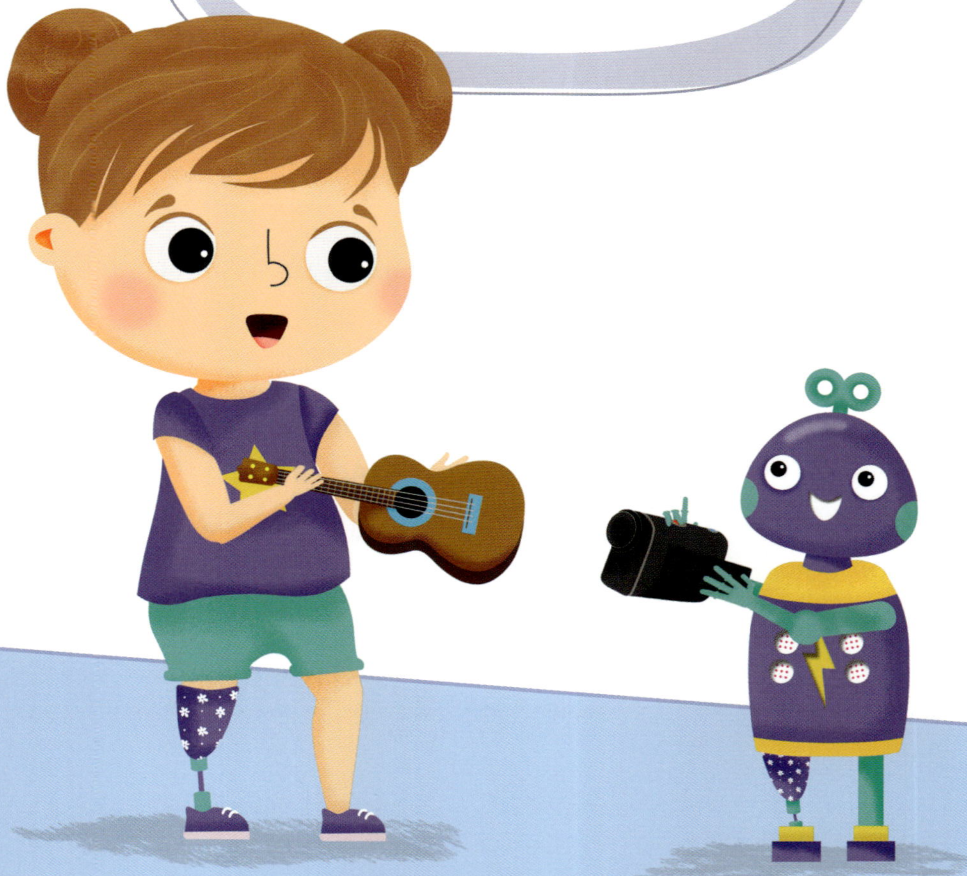

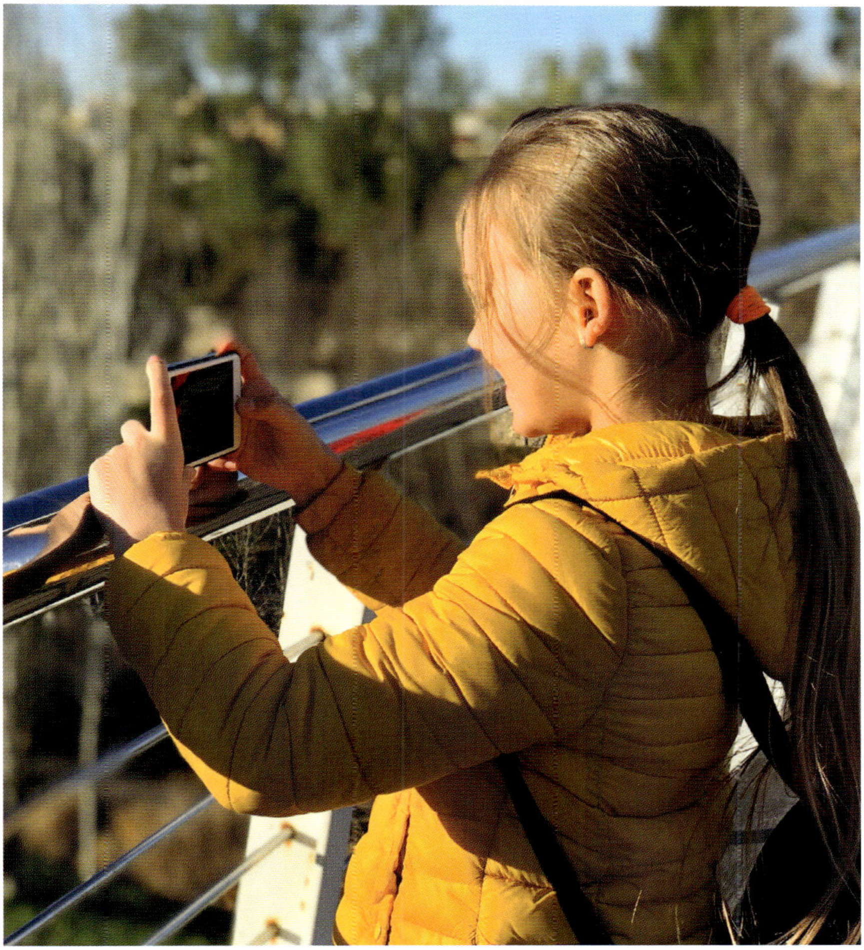

If you use a smartphone to record video, try using effects like slow motion.

CHAPTER THREE

Edit Your Video

After you finish filming your video, it's time to edit it. You can edit your video on the smartphone using a video-editing **app**. Or you can use a computer program like iMovie or Microsoft Photos. Be sure to ask an adult to help you **upload** your **footage** onto the computer.

There are many ways to edit your video. First, watch the video and cut out anything you don't want in your movie. These are called cuttakes. Maybe your actor forgot her lines. Maybe the camera was shaky during one scene. You can edit out these parts so they don't show up in the final video.

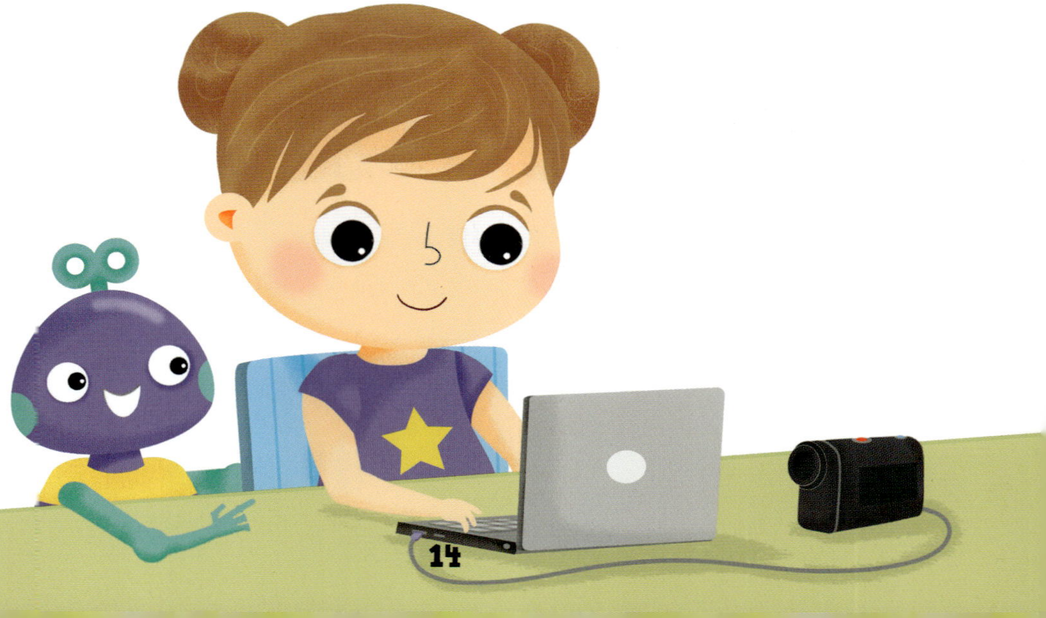

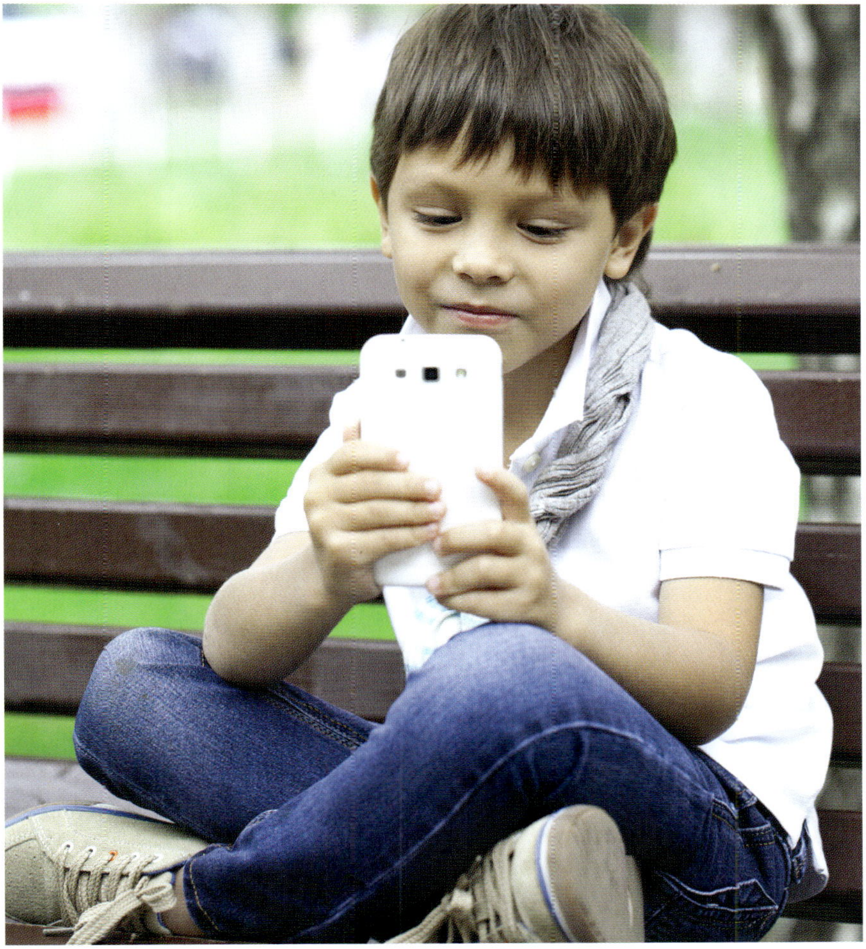

You might be able to use a smartphone to edit your video.

You can also do what movies and TV shows do. Add a title in the beginning and **credits** at the end. Some editing programs let you add cool effects or background music. Once you have cut your outtakes and added effects, save your movie on your computer. Now you are ready to share your video!

Adding music and effects can make your video even more fun!

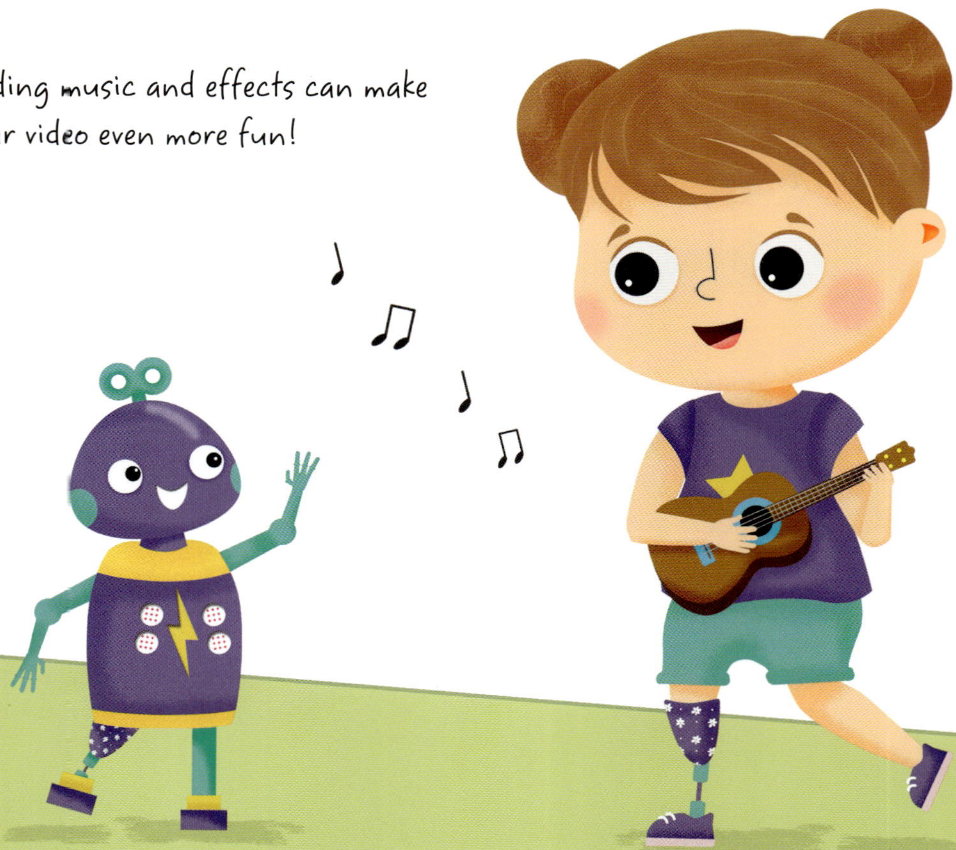

ACTIVITY

Edit Your Video

Now it's time to edit your video. This is where you can add in sound effects or cut out any **bloopers**!

INSTRUCTIONS:

1. Ask an adult to help you put your video on the computer. Or open your movie in a video-editing app on the phone.
2. Watch your footage to see what parts you want to keep.
3. Use the trimming tool to cut out the parts of your footage that you don't want.
4. If you need to, rearrange scenes so your video makes sense.
5. Now, add some cool effects and background music.
6. Give your video a title.
7. Add credits to your video.

TIP: Try editing the video on a computer using iMovie or Windows Photos.

CHAPTER FOUR

Share Your Video

Making videos isn't as fun without people to share them with! There are a lot of ways you can share your video. The easiest way is to invite your friends and family to watch your movie in a live **screening**. Make some popcorn and enjoy the show together!

What if you want to share your video with family members who don't live nearby? There are a lot of ways to share videos online! Your parents can help you upload a video to YouTube. But make sure that it is set to "unlisted." Then only the people with the link can see it. Or they can upload it to a website like Dropbox. They can invite family and friends to watch the video.

One way to show your movie is to gather people around your computer screen.

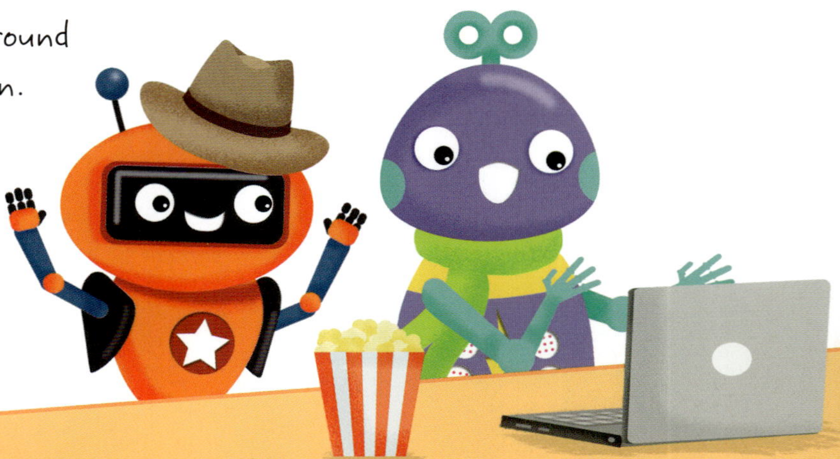

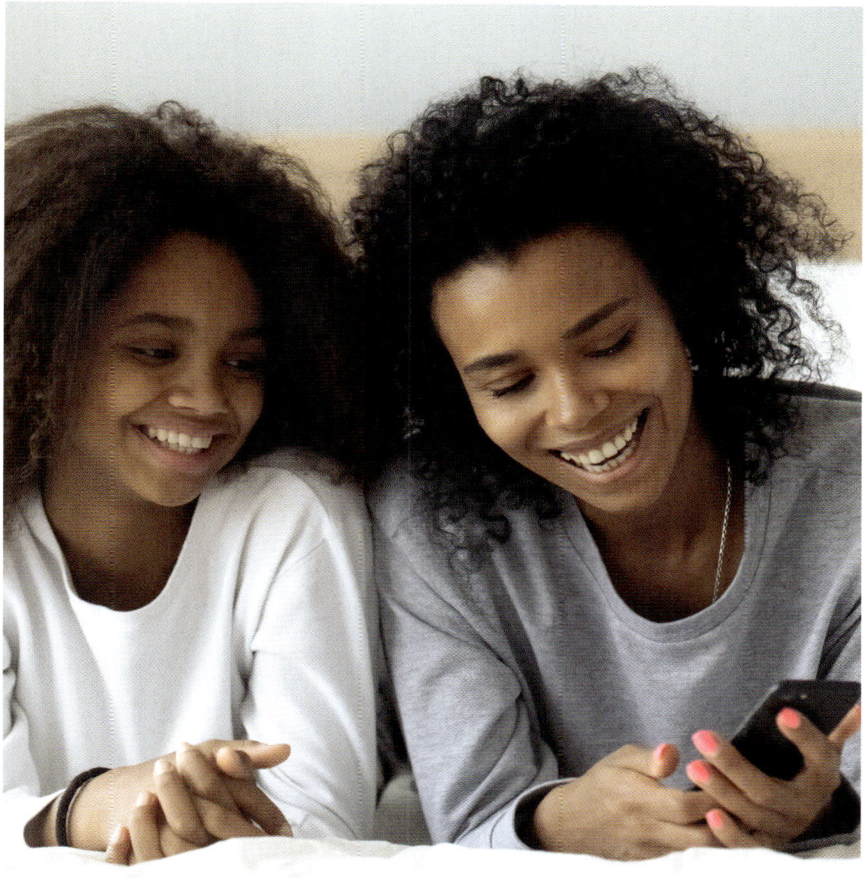

Don't post your video online without your parents' permission.

You might want to post your video on other websites, but it is important to be careful. Many social media sites let you share videos. But the law says you must be at least 13 years old to use these sites. You should always ask your parents what sites are safe for you to use to share your video.

Another way to share your video online is called livestreaming. You can't edit livestreamed video. It's best to ask your parents' permission before you make or watch any livestreamed videos.

ACTIVITY

Movie Review

Getting **feedback** on your video can help you improve! Ask your family and friends to answer these questions to help you make your next video even better:

- You did a really good job with . . . .
- One thing you can do better next time is . . . .
- I wonder what would happen if you . . . .
- Have you thought about . . . ?
- My favorite part was . . . .

Now that you have made your first video, it's time to reflect! What do you like about your movie? What do you wish you could change? The only way to improve is to keep trying.

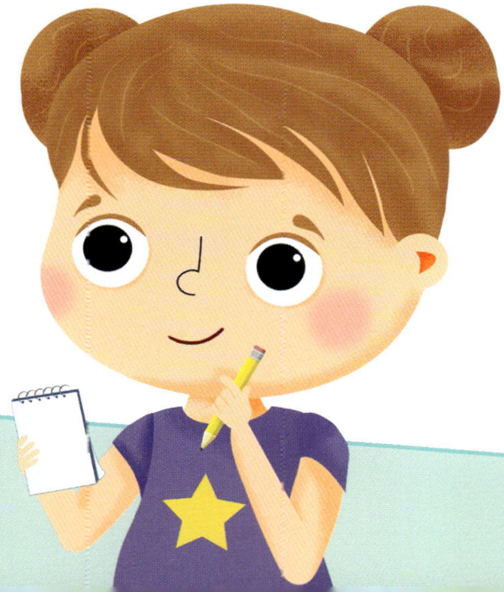

GLOSSARY

app (APP) a computer program, usually on a smartphone or tablet

audience (AW-dee-uhns) the people who view or read a movie, play, or book

bloopers (BLOO-purz) scenes containing a mistake

credits (KRED-itz) a list of names at the end of a movie or television program that tells you who made it

feedback (FEED-bak) reactions to something or comments about something

footage (FUT-ij) recorded video

inanimate (in-AN-uh-mit) not living

mood (MOOD) an emotional state of mind or feeling

props (PRAHPS) objects that are used to set the scene or used by actors, like a basketball or guitar

scenes (SEENZ) parts of a movie that show what is happening in particular places and times

screening (SKREEN-ing) an event held to show an audience a movie

script (SKRIPT) the written text of a movie

sequence (SEE-kwuhns) the order in which things happen or should happen

shots (SHAHTS) individual pieces of footage that are edited together to create scenes

storyboard (STOR-ee-bord) a visual plan of the shots a movie will include

upload (UHP-lohd) to send information from your computer to the internet

For More
INFORMATION

BOOK

Saldaña, Zoë Wilkinson. *Filming Stop-Motion Animation*. Ann Arbor, Michigan: Cherry Lake Publishing, 2018.

WEBSITES

Wonderopolis—How Many People Does It Take to Make a Movie?
https://www.wonderopolis.org/wonder/how-many-people-does-it-take-to-make-a-movie
Learn more about the moviemaking industry.

YouTube Kids
https://www.youtube.com/kids
Watch videos to get inspiration for your own movie.

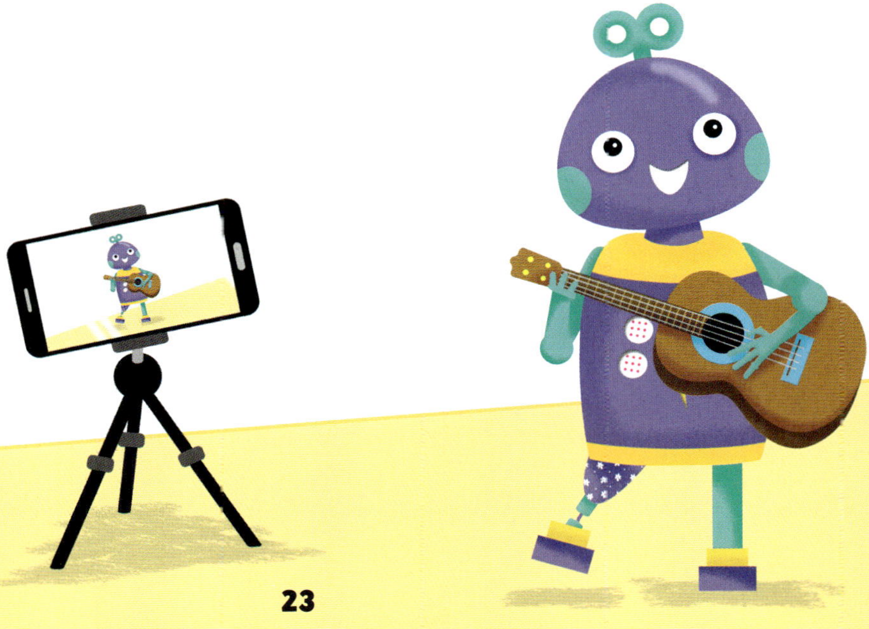

INDEX

About the AUTHOR

Amber Lovett is a certified school librarian and teacher. She lives with her husband, Karan, in Portland, Oregon.